● 101 RECIPES WITH CREAM CHEESE

D0040351

CREAM CHEESE
Cookbook

Printed in the USA by G&R Publishing Co., Waverly, IA

Published and distributed by:

507 Industrial Street
Waverly, IA 50677

ISBN-13: 978-1-56383-156-0
ISBN-10: 1-56383-156-2
Item #3715

Appetizers

Caramel Apple Dip

8 oz. cream cheese

¾ C. brown sugar

¾ C. white sugar

1 tsp. vanilla

Mix all ingredients. Dip apple slices in it.

Pickle Rolls

Ham lunch meat; make sure ham slices
    are not too thick or too thin

Dill pickles
Cream cheese

Take a slice of lunch meat; spread cream cheese on ham. Dry off dill pickle. Roll it up in the lunch meat and slice pickle up into several servings. Makes a great appetizer or snack.

Bread Pot Fondue

1 large loaf French bread, unsliced
2 C. Cheddar cheese, shredded
2-3 oz. pkgs. cream cheese, softened
1½ C. sour cream
1 C. cooked ham, diced

½ C. green onions, chopped
1 can green chilies, chopped
1 tsp. Worcestershire sauce
2 T. vegetable oil
1 T. butter, melted

Preheat oven to 350°. Slice off top of bread and save. Hollow out inside, leaving ½″ shell. Cut the hollowed-out bread in 1″ cubes. Combine Cheddar cheese, cream cheese and sour cream in bowl. Stir in ham, green onions, chilies and Worcestershire sauce. Spoon into bread. Replace top. Tightly wrap with double layers of foil; set on cookie sheet. Bake at 350° for 1 hour and 15 minutes, until cheese is melted and heated through. Stir together bread cubes, oil and melted butter. Arrange on cookie sheet; bake in 350° oven, turning occasionally, for 10 to 15 minutes, until golden brown. Use as dippers. When bread is done, remove top and stir filling before serving.

Salsa Dip

1 pkg. cream cheese
1 C. salsa

1 C. shredded Cheddar cheese

Mix well and serve with your favorite chip or tortilla chips.

Wedding Mints

1-8 oz. pkg. cream cheese	½ tsp. flavoring
1-2 lb. pkg. powdered sugar	Food coloring

Cream the cheese until soft. Add flavoring and food coloring. Beat with mixer, while adding powdered sugar. When it gets too firm for the mixer, turn out on counter (spread powdered sugar on counter first). Add more powdered sugar until a firm ball forms. Pinch off a small amount, roll in a ball and then roll in sugar. Press into a mold. Unmold onto a plate. Freeze until needed.

Cold Veggie Pizza

2 cans crescent rolls
2-8 oz. pkgs. cream cheese
1 env. ranch dressing
1 C. mayonnaise

Vegetables, chopped: broccoli,
cauliflower, peppers (green
or red), carrots
Onions, optional

Press crescent rolls on cookie sheet and pinch seams together. Bake for 10 minutes at 400°; let cool. Mix cream cheese, dressing and mayonnaise. Spread on top of crust. Chop (or use food processor) the vegetables. Sprinkle over top of crust. Tastes better if made ahead of time.

Hot Crab Dip

½ C. milk
⅓ C. salsa
3-8 oz. pkgs. cream cheese, cubed
2½-8 oz. pkgs. imitation crab meat,
   flaked

1 C. green onions, thinly sliced
1-4 oz. can green chilies,
   chopped
Assorted crackers

Combine milk and salsa. Transfer to slow cooker coated with cooking spray. Stir in cream cheese, crab, onions and chilies. Cover and cook on low about 3 hours, stirring often. Serve with crackers.

Fiesta Roll Ups

16 oz. sour cream
16 oz. cream cheese
2 (5 oz.) cans chunk ham
1 large onion

2 small cans chopped green
  chilies
1 C. chopped pecans
1 pkg. flour tortillas

Prepare the night before. Mix all ingredients except tortillas in large bowl. Spread on flour tortilla and roll. Set in refrigerator overnight. In the morning, cut into ¾″ pieces. Serve with picante sauce as garnish.

Corn Dip Olé

1-8 oz. pkg. cream cheese,
    softened
⅓ C. salsa

1-7 oz. can corn, drained
3 T. minced bell pepper
2 T. minced celery

Mix cream cheese and salsa in blender. Stir in corn, pepper and celery. Cover and refrigerate for 1 to 2 hours. Serve with tortilla chips.

Stuffed Bread

1½ lb. round dark bread, not sliced
1-8 oz. pkg. cream cheese, softened
1 C. sour cream

1-4 oz. can green chilies, chopped
1-2½ oz. pkg. dried beef
1½ C. shredded Cheddar cheese

Cut off top of bread and scoop out center. Break into pieces to be used to dip later. Mix remaining ingredients. Put dip mixture into hollow loaf. Wrap in foil. Bake at 300° for 1½ hours. Serve with broken bread pieces. As dip disappears, break bread shell and use to dip also.

Layered Shrimp Dip

8 oz. pkg. cream cheese
1 bottle chili sauce
3 or 4 green onions, chopped

½ C. chopped olives
1 can chopped shrimp, drained
4 oz. shredded mozzarella cheese

Layer the above ingredients in a pie plate in order given. Refrigerate until ready to serve. Serve with Doritos.

Hot Reuben Dip

2-8 oz. pkgs. cream cheese
1-8 oz. sour cream
1 small can sauerkraut

10 to 12 oz. corned beef
6 oz. shredded Swiss cheese
Party rye bread

Drain sauerkraut. Tear corned beef into small pieces. Mix all ingredients and heat in crock pot. Serve on party rye bread.

Crab Meat Rangoons

1 pkg. cream cheese
1 pkg. crab meat
2 T. fresh lemon juice
White pepper

4 x 4″ pasta wrap sheets
1 egg white
1 C. vegetable oil

Chop crab meat fine and mix with cream cheese, lemon juice, and the white pepper. Drop 1 tablespoon of the mixture into center of wrap. Fold and secure with egg. Seal carefully. Prepare oil by placing in a wok, deep-frying pan or deep fat fryer on medium-high heat. Drop rangoons in carefully and fry until golden brown on both sides. Remove from oil and drain. Serve hot.

Hot Beef-Mushroom Appetizer

2 medium onions, chopped
¼ C. butter or margarine
1-8 oz. pkg. cream cheese, softened
½ lb. fresh mushrooms, chopped

1-4½ oz. pkg. dried beef, chopped
½ tsp. Worcestershire sauce
½ tsp. garlic powder
Crackers or party rye bread

In a skillet, saute onions in butter until tender. Stir in cream cheese until smooth. Add mushrooms, beef, Worcestershire sauce and garlic powder; mix well. Spoon into a 9″ pie plate. Bake at 375° for 15 to 20 minutes. Serve warm with crackers or rye bread.

Hot Pizza Dip

1-8 oz. pkg. cream cheese, softened
1 tsp. Italian seasoning
1 C. (4 oz.) shredded mozzarella cheese

1-8 oz. can pizza sauce
2 T. chopped green pepper
2 T. thinly sliced onion
¾ C. grated Parmesan cheese
Breadsticks or tortilla chips

In a mixing bowl, beat cream cheese and Italian seasoning. Spread in an ungreased 9" microwave-safe pie plate. Combine mozzarella and Parmesan cheese; sprinkle half over the cream cheese. Top with the pizza sauce, remaining cheese mixture, green pepper and onion. Microwave, uncovered, on high for 3 to 4 minutes or until cheese is almost melted, rotating a half turn several times. Let stand for 1 to 2 minutes. Serve.

Fruit Pizza

¾ C. oleo
1½ C. flour
½ C. powdered sugar

TOPPING:
1-8 oz. pkg. cream cheese
½ C. powdered sugar
1 tsp. vanilla

Mix together oleo, flour and powdered sugar. Press in a pizza pan; bake at 350° for 15 minutes.

TOPPING: Mix together cream cheese, powdered sugar and vanilla; spread over crust. Arrange fruits (strawberries, mandarin oranges, pineapple tidbits, kiwi or grapes). Save 1 cup pineapple juice and add ½ cup sugar, 3 tablespoons cornstarch and 1 teaspoon lemon juice. Cook until clear; pour over top before serving.

Easy Dip

1-8 oz. pkg. cream cheese   1-15 oz. can chili, without beans

Combine ingredients and mix well. May be microwaved for a few minutes to melt the cheese slightly. Stir until blended. Serve warm or cold with deli chips, Fritos or crackers. For zip, add some jalapeno peppers.

Dried Beef Dip

2 small pkgs. cream cheese
1 small carton sour cream
1 pkg. dried beef
1 tsp. Worcestershire sauce

½ green pepper, minced
2 T. onion
¼ tsp. garlic salt
Slivered almonds

Mix well. Chop or cut dried beef in small pieces. Place in ovenproof dish. Sprinkle top with slivered almonds. Bake at 350° for 30 minutes or until bubbly. Serve with Triscuits or party rye.

Hot Italian Dip

1 lb. ground beef
½ C. chopped onion
1 clove garlic, crushed
1-8 oz. can tomato sauce

¼ C. catsup
1 tsp. oregano
8 oz. cream cheese, softened
½ C. Parmesan cheese

Cook ground beef, onion and garlic until beef is no longer pink; discard drippings. Mix ground beef mixture with tomato sauce, catsup and oregano in glass dish. Microwave on high for 5 minutes. Add cream cheese. Microwave on medium for 4 to 5 minutes or until cream cheese melts, stirring once. Stir in Parmesan cheese. Serve hot on rye bread or crackers.

Ribbon Pumpkin Bread

6 oz. cream cheese
¼ C. sugar

BATTER:
1 C. pumpkin
½ C. unsweetened applesauce
1 egg
2 egg whites
1 T. canola oil
1⅔ C. all-purpose flour

2 egg whites

1½ C. sugar
1 tsp. baking soda
½ tsp. salt
½ tsp. ground cinnamon
½ tsp. ground cloves
⅓ C. chopped walnuts

(continued on next page)

For filling, combine the cream cheese, sugar, flour and egg whites in a bowl; set aside. In a mixing bowl, beat the pumpkin, applesauce, egg, egg whites and oil. Combine the flour, sugar, baking soda, salt, cinnamon and cloves; add to pumpkin mixture. Stir in walnuts. Divide half of the batter between two 8 x 4 x 2″ loaf pans coated with nonstick cooking spray. Spread each with filling. Top with remaining batter. Bake at 350° for 40 to 45 minutes or until a toothpick inserted near the center comes out clean. Cool for 10 minutes before removing from pans to wire racks to cool completely. Refrigerate leftovers.

Creamy Chicken Spread

1½ C. chopped, cooked chicken
1-8 oz. pkg. cream cheese, softened
½ C. chopped celery
½ C. mayonnaise

2 T. chopped onion
1 tsp. onion powder
½ tsp. salt

Place all ingredients in a food processor; process until coarsely chopped. Use as a sandwich spread or serve on crackers.

Broiled-Tomato Bagels

4 bagels, split
½ C. herbed cream cheese
½ C. spinach leaves

1 tomato, thinly sliced
1 red onion, thinly sliced

Preheat oven to 350°. Line a baking sheet with foil. Place bagel halves, cut side up, on sheet. Spread each half with 1 tablespoon cream cheese. Then top with spinach, tomatoes and onion slices. Bake until bagels begin to brown and are heated through, 5 to 8 minutes.

Championship Bean Dip

1-16 oz. can refried beans
1 C. picante sauce
1 C. (4 oz.) shredded Monterey
    Jack cheese
1 C. (4 oz.) shredded Cheddar
    cheese

¾ C. sour cream
1-3 oz. pkg. cream cheese,
    softened
1 T. chili powder
¼ tsp. ground cumin

In a bowl, combine the first eight ingredients; transfer to a slow cooker. Cover and cook on high for 2 hours or until heated through, stirring once or twice. Serve with tortilla chips.

Dairy Delicious Dip

1-8 oz. pkg. cream cheese,
   softened
½ C. sour cream

¼ C. sugar
¼ C. brown sugar
1 to 2 T. maple syrup

In a small mixing bowl, combine cream cheese, sour cream, sugars and syrup to taste; beat until smooth. Chill. Serve with fresh fruit.

Zippy French Bread

6 oz. cream cheese, softened
¼ C. butter, softened
2 T. minced chives

3 tsp. horseradish
1-1 lb. loaf French bread

In a small bowl, beat cream cheese, butter, chives and horseradish until well mixed. Cut bread 1″ thick, half from bottom of loaf. Spread cream cheese mixture between slices. Wrap loaf in foil. Bake at 400° for 15 minutes.

Awesome Cucumber Dip

½ C. grated cucumber
2 T. grated onion
1 tsp. garlic powder

8 oz. cream cheese
¼ C. mayonnaise

Peel cucumber, split down the middle and scoop out the seeds with a spoon. Grate it, and when finished, squeeze all excess water out. Add other ingredients and mix. Serve on crackers or rye party bread.

Blue Cheese Ball

2-3 oz. pkgs. cream cheese
1½ oz. blue cheese
1-5 oz. jar smoke cheese spread
1 T. Worcestershire sauce

1 T. minced onion
2 T. parsley flakes
1 T. stuffed olives, chopped fine
½ C. finely chopped pecans

Combine all ingredients except chopped pecans; blend well and chill. Form into one or two balls as desired. Roll in chopped pecans. Chill again before serving. Serve with crackers. Freezes well.

Fruit Dip

1-8 oz. pkg. cream cheese,
  softened
2-7 oz. cartons marshmallow creme

½ tsp. cinnamon
⅛ tsp. ground ginger

With mixer, combine and beat together all ingredients. Mix well. Refrigerate. Serve with unpeeled slices of apples, strawberries, nectarines, etc.

Taco Dip

FIRST LAYER:
1 lb. hamburger
1 can refried beans
1 pkg. taco seasoning

SECOND LAYER:
8 oz. cream cheese
½ jar taco sauce

THIRD LAYER:
Shredded cheese

Bake at 350° until cheese melts. Dip in chips.

Hot Crab Meat Appetizer

1-8 oz. pkg. cream cheese,
    softened
1-7½ oz. can crab meat, drained
    and flaked
2 T. finely chopped onion

2 T. milk
½ tsp. cream-style horseradish
¼ tsp. salt
Dash of pepper
⅓ C. sliced almonds, toasted

Combine all ingredients except almonds, mixing until well blended. Spoon mixture into a 9″ pie plate. Sprinkle with almonds. Bake at 375° for 15 minutes. Serve with crackers.

Artichoke Dip

1-4 oz. jar artichoke hearts, drained
¼ C. parsley
8 oz. cream cheese, softened
½ C. sour cream

2 cloves garlic, pressed
Salt and pepper to taste
Squeeze of lemon juice
½ C. chopped sunflower seeds
1 T. Parmesan cheese

Chop the artichoke hearts finely with parsley; set aside. Mix cream cheese with sour cream, Parmesan cheese, garlic, salt, pepper and lemon juice. Add artichoke mixture to cream cheese mixture. Add sunflower seeds; blend well. Serve with crackers or vegetables.

Mexican Roll-Ups

1-8 oz. cream cheese
1-8 oz. sour cream
1 pkg. dry Italian seasoning mix
10 large flour tortillas

2 carrots, grated
1 red pepper, chopped
1 green pepper, chopped
5 or 6 green onions, chopped

Mix together cream cheese, sour cream and seasoning. Spread this mixture nearly to edge of tortillas. Sprinkle with carrots, peppers and onions. Roll up and refrigerate at least 2 hours. When ready, slice.

VARIATION: May use other vegetables.

Olive Dip

1-8 oz. cream cheese, softened
1 stick margarine, softened
2 T. green olive juice

1 jar green olives, cut up
2 small cans sliced black
   olives

Mix all ingredients thoroughly in order. Chill.

Dried Beef Roll-Ups

1 pkg. dried beef
1-8 oz. pkg. cream cheese

Minced chives or onion

Make a layer of dried beef about 4 x 4". Mix cream cheese and minced chives or onions. Spread on softened cheese mixture. Make three layers, ending with cheese. Roll up like a jelly roll, wrap in wax paper and refrigerate overnight. Slice and serve on Ritz crackers.

Pepperoni Pizza Dip

1-8 oz. cream cheese
1-8 oz. sour cream

1 jar pizza sauce
Pepperoni, chopped small

Mix cream cheese and sour cream together. Pour into a 9″ pie pan. Spread pizza sauce over the mixture. Top with pepperoni. Bake at 350° until bubbly. Serve with tortilla chips or crackers.

Cheese Spread

1 lb. Velveeta
8 oz. cream cheese
½ C. Western dressing
½ C. mayonnaise or Miracle Whip

1 small bunch green onions
1 green pepper
2 pkgs. dried beef

Melt Velveeta (this works great in the microwave). With electric mixer, beat cream cheese until softened. Mix in Western dressing and mayonnaise. Add melted Velveeta and beat until smooth and creamy. Chop green onions, green pepper and dried beef. Combine with cheese mixture (do not use electric mixer). Serve spread with crackers.

Salads & Veggies

24-Hour Salad

1-8 oz. pkg. cream cheese
¼ C. salad dressing
1-20 oz. can crushed pineapple,
    drained

½ pkg. miniature marshmallows
1-8 oz. tub whipped topping
Chopped nuts
Maraschino cherries

Cream the cream cheese and salad dressing together. Add the crushed pineapple, miniature marshmallows and whipped topping. Pour and spread in a long, flat glass dish. Top with chopped nuts and cut-up maraschino cherries. Refrigerate 24 hours. Cut into squares and serve.

Frozen Fruit Salad

½ C. cherries, halved
2-3 oz. pkgs. cream cheese
¼ C. mayonnaise

1 can fruit cocktail, drained
2 C. whipped topping
2½ C. marshmallows

Blend cream cheese with mayonnaise. Add a few drops of cherry juice. Add rest of ingredients and mix well. Pour mix into mold and freeze.

Autumn Apple Salad

1-20 oz. can crushed pineapple,
    undrained
⅔ C. sugar
1-3 oz. pkg. lemon gelatin
1-8 oz. pkg. cream cheese

1 C. diced, unpeeled apples
½ C. chopped nuts
1 C. chopped celery
1 C. whipped topping

In saucepan, combine pineapple and sugar; bring to a boil and boil 3 minutes. Add gelatin; stir until dissolved. Add cream cheese; stir until thoroughly combined. Cool. Fold in apples, nuts, celery and whipped topping. Pour in 9″ square pan. Chill until firm and cut in squares.

Seafoam Salad

3 small pkgs. lime jello
3 C. pear juice
2-29 oz. cans pears

8 oz. cream cheese, softened
8 oz. whipped topping, softened
4 T. milk

Heat pear juice to a boil; pour over jello. Cream the cheese with the milk and add to the jello, along with 3 cups of cold water. Let mixture cool and thicken slightly. Mash pears with a fork, then add to jello mixture. Blend in whipped topping. Spread in 9 x 13″ pan and allow to set.

Red, White and Blue Salad

FIRST LAYER:
2 boxes raspberry jello

3½ C. hot water

SECOND LAYER:
1 pkg. unflavored gelatin
½ C. cold water

1 C. milk
1 C. sugar

THIRD LAYER:
1 box raspberry jello
1 C. hot water

1-#303 can blueberries,
   juice and all

(continued on next page)

FIRST LAYER: Mix and let set.

SECOND LAYER: Dissolve gelatin in cold water. Heat milk and sugar to boiling; do not boil.

ADD:

½ C. nuts	1-8 oz. pkg. cream cheese,
1 tsp. vanilla	softened

Combine above ingredients and partially set before pouring over first layer.

THIRD LAYER: Let partially set and pour over second layer.

Creamy Frozen Fruit Cups

1-8 oz. pkg. cream cheese,
  softened
½ C. sugar
1-10 oz. jar maraschino cherries,
  drained
1-11 oz. can mandarin oranges,
  drained

1-8 oz. can crushed pineapple,
  drained
½ C. pecans, chopped
1-8 oz. carton frozen whipped
  topping, thawed
Fresh mint, optional

In a mixing bowl, beat the cream cheese and sugar until fluffy. Halve 9 cherries; chop the remaining cherries. Reserve 18 oranges for garnish. Add the pineapple, pecans and chopped cherries to cream cheese mixture. Fold in whipped topping and remaining oranges. Line muffin cups with paper or foil liners. Spoon fruit mixture into cups; garnish with reserved cherries and oranges. Freeze until firm. Remove from freezer 10 minutes before serving. Top with mint, if desired.

Fresh and Creamy Potato Salad

4 C. cubed, cooked potatoes
½ C. celery, sliced
¼ C. chopped green pepper
2 T. green onion slices
1 tsp. salt

1-8 oz. pkg. cream cheese,
   softened
½ C. sour cream
2 T. milk

Combine potatoes, celery, green peppers, onion and salt; mix lightly. Combine cream cheese, sour cream and milk, mixing until well blended. Add to potato mixture; mix lightly. Chill.

Broccoli with Rich Cheese Sauce

2 T. melted butter
2 T. all-purpose flour
1-3 oz. pkg. cream cheese,
    softened
1-1 oz. piece blue cheese, crumbled

1 C. milk
2-10 oz. pkgs. chopped
    broccoli
⅓ C. crushed crackers

Cook and drain broccoli according to directions on package. In large saucepan, blend butter, flour, cream cheese and blue cheese. Add milk slowly; cook and stir until bubbly. Stir in cooked broccoli. Turn into 1-quart casserole. Top with cracker crumbs. Bake at 350° for 25 minutes.

Creamy Broccoli Cabbage

4 C. shredded cabbage
½ lb. fresh broccoli florets
2 T. butter

4 oz. cream cheese, cubed
Salt and pepper

Place cabbage and broccoli in a saucepan; add 1″ of water and bring to a boil. Reduce heat; cover and simmer 8 to 10 minutes. In another pan, melt butter. Stir in cream cheese until melted. Drain vegetables well. Top with butter and cream cheese. Salt and pepper to taste.

Cheesy Creamed Corn

3-16 oz. pkgs. frozen corn
1-8 oz. pkg. cream cheese, cubed
1-3 oz. pkg. cream cheese, cubed
¼ C. margarine, cubed
3 T. water

3 T. milk
2 T. sugar
6 slices process American cheese,
    cut in small pieces

Combine all ingredients in a slow cooker; mix well. Cover and cook on low for 4 hours or until heated through and cheese is melted. Stir well before serving.

Potato and Broccoli Supreme

3 C. mashed potatoes (5 or 6)
1-3 oz. pkg. cream cheese
¼ C. milk
1 egg
2 T. butter

Salt and pepper, to taste
1 can French fried onions
2-10 oz. pkgs. frozen broccoli,
    cooked and drained
1 C. shredded cheese

Mix first five ingredients together and season with salt and pepper to taste. Fold in half the can of French fried onions. Press mixture into the bottom a greased 9 x 13″ baking dish. Bake at 350° for 25 to 30 minutes. Arrange cooked broccoli in baked potato shell and sprinkle with shredded cheese and remaining French fried onions. Bake, uncovered, for an additional 5 minutes.

Creamy Potatoes

8 to 10 potatoes
8 oz. sour cream
Parsley flakes, optional

8 oz. cream cheese
Paprika, optional
Grated cheese, optional

Cook the peeled potatoes; drain. Whip 1 potato in a large mixing bowl and add the cream cheese. Continue whipping and adding potatoes, a few at a time. When half the potatoes have been whipped, add the sour cream and continue whipping. Continue adding potatoes until all are whipped, fluffy and smooth. Put in buttered casserole. May be baked immediately, refrigerated, or frozen for later use. Top with paprika, parsley flakes or grated cheese, if desired. Baking time varies on when they are used. Bake at 325° for a glass container, 350° for a metal.

Baked Mashed Potatoes

8 to 10 potatoes, boiled and
    mashed
1 tsp. garlic salt
1-8 oz. pkg. cream cheese

1 carton (½ pt.) sour cream
¼ C. grated onion
¼ C. butter
2 tsp. paprika

Whip cheese and sour cream until smooth. Add garlic salt and onion. Add potatoes while hot and whip. Put in buttered casserole and dot with butter on top. Sprinkle with paprika. Bake at 350° for 45 minutes.

Homespun Scalloped Potatoes

1-8 oz. cream cheese, cubed
1¼ C. milk
½ tsp. salt

⅛ tsp. pepper
4 C. thin potato slices
2 T. chopped chives

In large saucepan, combine cream cheese, milk, salt and pepper. Stir over low heat until smooth. Add potatoes and chives; mix lightly. Spoon into 1½-quart casserole; cover. Bake at 350° for 1 hour and 10 minutes or until potatoes are tender. Stir before serving.

Gourmet Potatoes

10 medium potatoes	1 tsp. salt
¼ C. margarine	Dash of onion salt
¾ C. milk	or flakes
1-3 oz. pkg. cream cheese	½ C. sour cream

Cook potatoes and whip with margarine, salt, onion salt and milk. Add sour cream and cream cheese. Continue whipping until smooth. Place in refrigerator. To serve, place in oven at 325° for 30 minutes. Fluffiness remains good as twice baked; freezes well.

Creamy Mashed Potatoes

8 to 10 potatoes
1-8 oz. pkg. cream cheese
1 stick butter

1 C. milk
Seasoning salt

Clean and peel potatoes. Boil potatoes until soft. Drain water and place potatoes in mixing bowl. Add cream cheese, butter and milk. Mix together. Season to taste.

Main Dishes

Savory Scrambled Eggs

2 T. margarine
6 eggs, beaten
⅓ C. milk

Salt and pepper
1-3 oz. pkg. cream cheese, cubed

Melt margarine in skillet over low heat; add combined eggs, milk and seasonings. Cook slowly, stirring until eggs begin to thicken. Add cream cheese; continue cooking, stirring occasionally, until cream cheese is melted and eggs are cooked.

Breakfast Bread Pudding

12 slices white bread   2 C. milk
1-8 oz. pkg. cream cheese, cubed   ⅓ C. maple syrup
12 eggs   ¼ tsp. salt

Remove and discard crusts from bread. Cut bread into cubes. Toss lightly with cream cheese cubes. Place in a greased 13 x 9 x 2″ baking pan. In a large mixing bowl, beat eggs. Add milk, syrup and salt; pour over bread mixture. Cover and refrigerate 8 hours or overnight. Remove from refrigerator 30 minutes before baking. Bake uncovered at 375° for 40 to 45 minutes or until knife inserted near the center comes out clean. Let stand 5 minutes before cutting.

Ultimate Grilled Cheese Sandwich

1-3 oz. pkg. cream cheese
½ C. mayonnaise
1 C. Cheddar cheese, shredded
1 C. mozzarella cheese, shredded

½ tsp. garlic powder
¼ tsp. seasoning salt
10 slices Italian bread
2 T. butter or oleo

Combine first six ingredients; spread on 5 bread slices. Top with another bread slice. Melt oleo in skillet and fry sandwich on each side until golden brown.

Creamy Fettuccine Alfredo

1-8 oz. pkg. cream cheese
¾ C. grated Parmesan cheese
½ C. margarine

½ C. milk
8 oz. fettuccine, cooked and
    drained

In large saucepan, combine cream cheese, Parmesan cheese, margarine and milk;
stir over low heat until smooth. Add hot fettuccine; toss lightly.

Cream of Broccoli Soup

1 lb. broccoli or cauliflower
¼ lb. butter or margarine
4 to 5 T. flour, mixed in 2 C. milk
3 C. water

2 medium onions, diced
3 chicken bouillon cubes
1-8 oz. pkg. cream cheese

Boil vegetables until done with onion, margarine and bouillon cubes. Then add milk-flour mixture along with cream cheese. Stir slowly until thick.

Potato Soup

3 to 4 C. diced potatoes
1 C. sliced celery
1 C. shredded carrots
Diced onion, to your taste
8 C. milk

Salt and pepper, to taste
¼ C. margarine
1 can cream of chicken soup
1-8 oz. pkg. cream cheese

Boil potatoes, carrots, celery and onion; drain. Add remaining ingredients and cook until heated through.

Mexican Pizza

2-8 oz. tubes refrigerated crescent
    rolls
1-8 oz. pkg. cream cheese
1 C. sour cream
1 lb. ground beef
1 env. taco seasoning mix

1-2¼ oz. can sliced ripe olives,
    drained
1 medium tomato, chopped
¾ C. shredded Cheddar cheese
¾ C. shredded mozzarella cheese
1 C. shredded lettuce

Unroll crescent roll dough and place in an ungreased 15 x 10 x 1″ baking pan. Flatten dough to fit the pan, sealing seams and perforations. Bake at 375° for 8 to 10 minutes or until light golden brown; cool. In a small bowl, blend cream cheese and sour cream with a wire whisk. Spread over crust. Chill 30 minutes. Meanwhile, in a skillet, brown beef; drain. Stir in taco seasoning. Add water according to package directions and simmer for 5 minutes, stirring occasionally. Spread over cream cheese layer. Top with olives, tomato, cheeses and lettuce. Cut into serving-size pieces.

Four Cheese Manicotti

12 uncooked manicotti	1 tsp. dried Italian seasoning
Cooking spray	½ tsp. pepper
½ C. chopped onion	1-15 oz. carton ricotta cheese
3 garlic cloves, minced	1-6 oz. pkg. chopped spinach,
1 C. shredded mozzarella cheese,	thawed and drained
divided	1-6 oz. cream cheese
½ C. Parmesan cheese, divided	1-27½ oz. jar tomato sauce

Cook pasta; set aside. Sauté onion and garlic on medium heat for 3 minutes with cooking spray. In another bowl, combine ½ cup mozzarella cheese, ¼ cup Parmesan cheese, Italian seasoning, pepper, ricotta cheese, spinach and cream cheese. Mix with a mixer at medium speed or beat until smooth. Stir in onion and garlic. Spoon mixture into cooked manicotti (about ½ cup per shell). Place in a 9 x 13″ baking dish. Pour sauce over the top of the noodles. Sprinkle with remaining mozzarella and Parmesan cheese. Bake at 350° for 45 minutes.

Pasta in Tomatoes

1 C. bow tie pasta
4 large fresh tomatoes
¼ C. sliced green onion
1 garlic clove, minced
1 T. basil

1 T. butter
1-3 oz. cream cheese, cubed
¼ C. mozzarella, shredded
¼ C. grated Parmesan
⅛ tsp. ground pepper

Cook pasta. Slice tomatoes in half. Scoop out insides of tomatoes. Mix pasta, onion, garlic, basil, butter and the cheeses together. Fill each half of tomato with pasta mixture. Sprinkle with ground pepper.

Bacon-Wrapped Chicken

6 boneless, skinless chicken
   breast halves
1-8 oz. carton whipped cream
   cheese with onion and chives

1 T. butter or margarine, cubed
Salt to taste
6 bacon strips

Flatten chicken to ½″ thickness. Spread 3 tablespoons cream cheese over each. Dot with butter and sprinkle with salt. Roll up. Wrap each with a bacon strip. Place, seam side down, in a greased 13 x 9″ baking pan. Bake, uncovered, at 400° for 35 to 40 minutes or until juices run clear. Broil 6″ from heat for 5 minutes until bacon is crisp.

Fast and Easy Chicken

4 chicken breasts
1 pkg. Good Seasons dry salad
　　dressing
¼ C. water

1 can cream of mushroom
　　soup
8 oz. cream cheese
1 can mushrooms

Cook chicken, salad dressing and water in crock pot until done. Blend other ingredients; pour over chicken and cook another hour. Serve with rice or noodles.

Savory Chicken Crescent Squares

8 oz. can crescent rolls
3 oz. cream cheese, softened
2 T. butter, melted
2 C. cooked, cubed chicken
¼ tsp. salt

⅛ tsp. pepper
2 T. milk
1 T. onion
1 T. pimiento

Use fingers to press out cut line in crescent rolls until you have four squares. Blend cream cheese and butter until smooth. Add all other ingredients together and mix. Fill square with ½ cup of mixture. Bring corners to top and close. Brush with melted butter. Bake as directed for rolls.

Desserts

Cream Cheese Frosting

1-8 oz. pkg. cream cheese
½ C. butter, softened

2 tsp. vanilla
4 C. powdered sugar

Place cheese and butter over low heat; soften. Add sugar and vanilla. Mix until smooth. Ready to use, or refrigerator for later.

Creamy Peach Dessert

½ C. milk
3 T. butter or margarine, melted
1 egg
¾ C. flour
1-3 oz. pkg. cook-and-serve vanilla
    pudding mix

TOPPING:
2-8 oz. pkgs. cream cheese,
    softened
¾ C. plus 1 T. sugar, divided

1 tsp. baking powder
½ tsp. salt
4 to 5 medium ripe peaches,
    peeled and sliced

⅓ C. half and half cream
1/2 tsp. ground cinnamon

(continued on next page)

In a mixing bowl, beat the milk, butter and egg. Combine the flour, pudding mix, baking powder and salt; add to milk mixture. Beat on medium speed for 2 minutes. Pour into a greased 8″ square baking dish. Top with peaches. In a small mixing bowl, beat cream cheese, ¾ cup sugar and cream. Drop by tablespoonfuls over peaches. Combine the cinnamon and remaining sugar; sprinkle over the top. Bake at 350° for 55 to 60 minutes or until puffed and golden brown. Cool on wire rack for 1 hour. Refrigerate for at least 2 hours before cutting.

Cream Puff Dessert

½ C. butter
1 C. flour
1 C. water
4 eggs
3 small pkgs. instant vanilla pudding

3 C. milk
1-8 oz. pkg. cream cheese
1-8 oz. carton whipped topping
Chocolate syrup

Preheat oven to 400°. Bring butter and water to a boil. Remove from heat and add flour. Add eggs, one at a time, beating after each. Mixture will form a ball. Pat in lightly greased 10 x 15″ pan. Bake 30 to 35 minutes, until lightly browned. Remove from oven and lightly press down. Let cool. Mix pudding and milk (2¾ cups). Add cream cheese that has been mixed with the other ¼ cup milk. Spread over cooled crust. Spread whipped topping over pudding and drizzle with chocolate syrup.

Chocolate Chip Cream Cheese Bars

1-18 oz. tube refrigerated chocolate
   chip cookie dough
1-8 oz. cream cheese, softened

½ C. sugar
1 egg

Take half of the cookie dough and press into the bottom of a greased 8″ pan. In a bowl, beat cream cheese, egg and sugar until smooth. Spread over crust. Crumble remaining dough over top. Bake at 350° for 35 to 40 minutes. Refrigerate leftovers.

Easy Cherry Tarts

1-8 oz. tube refrigerated crescent
    rolls
1-3 oz. pkg. cream cheese,
    softened

¼ C. confectioners' sugar
1 C. canned cherry pie
    filling
½ tsp. almond extract

Place crescent dough on a lightly floured surface; seal seams and perforations. Cut into 2″ circles. Place in greased miniature muffin cups. In small mixing bowl, beat cream cheese and confectioners' sugar until smooth. Place about ½ teaspoon in each cup. Combine pie filling and extract; place about 2 teaspoons in each cup. Bake at 375° for 12 to 14 minutes or until edges are lightly brown. Remove to wire racks to cool.

Cold Oven Pound Cake

3 sticks butter
6 eggs
3 C. flour

8 oz. pkg. cream cheese
3 C. sugar
1 tsp. vanilla

Cream butter, cream cheese and sugar. Beat in eggs, one at a time. Add flour and vanilla. Place in a cold oven. Heat oven to 300° and bake 1½ hours. Serve with fresh fruit.

Butterfinger Cake

1 German chocolate cake mix
1 large pkg. vanilla pudding or
    2 small pkgs.

8 oz. cream cheese
1⅓ C. milk

Mix, bake and cool cake. Beat remaining ingredients and put on cooled cake. Add small carton of whipped topping and top with 3 Butterfinger candy bars, crushed.

Petite Cherry Cheesecake

2-8 oz. pkgs. cream cheese,
    softened
¾ C. sugar
1 T. lemon juice

1 tsp. vanilla
24 vanilla wafers
1-21 oz. can cherry pie filling
2 eggs

Beat cream cheese, sugar, eggs, lemon juice and vanilla until light and fluffy. Line with paper cups in muffin tins. Fill two-thirds full of cheese mixture. Bake in 375° oven for 15 to 20 minutes, or until set. Top each with 1 tablespoon cherry pie filling.

Marbled Brownies

Brownie mix
2-3 oz. pkgs. cream cheese
5 T. margarine
⅓ C. sugar

5 eggs
2 T. flour
¾ tsp. vanilla

Soften cream cheese and margarine; beat together. Add sugar and 2 eggs, flour and vanilla. Beat until smooth; set aside. Mix by hand the brownie mix, 2 tablespoons water and 3 eggs. Pour half of batter into greased 9 x 13″ pan. Pour all of cream cheese mixture over batter. Spoon rest of brownie mixture over top. Pull knife through to marble. Bake at 350° for 35 to 40 minutes.

Raspberry Ribbon Pie

1-3 oz. pkg. raspberry jello
¼ C. sugar
1¼ C. boiling water
1-10 oz. pkg. frozen red raspberries
1 tsp. lemon juice
1-3 oz. pkg. cream cheese, softened

⅓ C. powdered sugar
1 tsp. vanilla
Dash of salt
1 C. whipped cream
1-9″ pie shell (bake until brown,
    then cool)

RED LAYER: Dissolve jello and sugar in the boiling water. Add frozen red raspberries and lemon juice; stir until berries thaw. Chill until partially set.

WHITE LAYER: Meanwhile, blend well the cream cheese, powdered sugar, vanilla and salt. Fold in a small amount of whipped cream, then fold in remainder. Spread half the white cheese mixture over the bottom of pie shell. Cover with half the red jello mixture. Repeat layers. Chill until set.

10-Minute German Sweet
Chocolate Cream Pie

1-4 oz. pkg. Baker's German
    sweet chocolate
½ C. milk, divided
2 T. sugar
1-3 oz. pkg. cream cheese, softened

3½ C. or 1-8 oz. container
    whipped topping, thawed
8″ graham cracker crumb
    crust

Heat chocolate and 2 tablespoons of the milk in saucepan over low heat, stirring until chocolate is melted. Beat sugar into cream cheese; add remaining milk and chocolate mixture and beat until smooth. Fold in whipped topping, blending until smooth. Spoon into crust. Freeze until firm, about 4 hours. Garnish with chocolate curls, if desired. Store any leftover pie in freezer.

CHOCOLATE MINT PIE: Prepare pie as directed above, adding ¼ teaspoon peppermint extract to chocolate-cream cheese mixture.

Chocolate Fudge

4 C. sifted confectioners' sugar
1-8 oz. pkg. cream cheese
4-1 oz. squares unsweetened
   chocolate, melted

1 tsp. vanilla
½ C. chopped nuts

Gradually add sugar to softened cream cheese, mixing until well blended. Stir in remaining ingredients. Spread into 8″ square pan. Chill several hours or overnight. Cut into squares.

Kiwifruit Danish

1-3 oz. pkg. refrigerator crescent
    dinner rolls
1-3 oz. pkg. cream cheese, softened
1 egg yolk

2 T. sugar
½ C. apricot jam
2 to 3 kiwifruit, pared and sliced
½ tsp. almond extract

Unroll crescent roll dough and shape into eight triangles with equal sides. Combine cream cheese, egg yolk, sugar and almond extract; blend well. Place 1 tablespoon cream cheese mixture in center of each triangle; top with kiwifruit slice. Pull points of triangle to center and pinch to seal. Bake on greased baking sheet at 375° for 12 to 15 minutes or until golden brown. Cool on rack. Heat jam. Top each Danish with another kiwifruit slice; brush with jam.

Dream Layer Surprise

1 stick softened butter
1 C. flour
¼ C. chopped pecans
8 oz. pkg. cream cheese
1 large whipped topping, divided
1 C. powdered sugar

1 small pkg. instant chocolate
    pudding
1 small pkg. instant vanilla
    pudding
4 Heath candy bars

Mix butter, flour and pecans. Pat in 13 x 9″ pan and bake 15 minutes at 325°. Mix cream cheese, 1 cup whipped topping and powdered sugar. Spread over first layer. Mix chocolate pudding and spread over cream cheese layer. Mix vanilla pudding; spread over top. Spread rest of whipped topping over vanilla pudding. Crush 4 Heath candy bars and sprinkle on top.

Chocolate Pudding Pizza

1-17½ oz. peanut butter cookie mix
1-12 oz. carton softened cream cheese
1¾ C. cold milk
1-3.9 oz. pkg. instant chocolate
    pudding mix

1-8 oz. carton frozen whipped
    topping, thawed
¼ C. miniature semi-sweet
    chocolate chips

Prepare cookie mix dough according to package directions. Press into a greased 12″ pizza pan. Bake at 375° for 15 minutes or until set. Cool. In a mixing bowl, beat cream cheese until smooth; spread over crust. In another mixing bowl, beat milk and pudding mix on medium speed for 2 minutes. Spread over cream cheese layer. Refrigerate for 20 minutes or until set. Spread with whipped topping. Sprinkle with chips. Chill for 1 to 2 hours.

Creamy Peanut Butter Pie

CRUST:
1¼ C. chocolate cookie crumbs
    (20 cookies)
¼ C. sugar
¼ C. butter, melted

FILLING:
1-8 oz. pkg. cream cheese, softened
1 C. creamy peanut butter
1 C. sugar
1 T. butter, softened
1 tsp. vanilla
1 C. heavy cream, whipped

Combine crust ingredients; press into a 9″ pie plate. Bake at 375° for 10 minutes. Cool. In a mixing bowl, beat cream cheese, peanut butter, sugar, butter and vanilla until smooth. Fold in whipped cream. Gently spoon into crust. Garnish with grated chocolate or cookie crumbs if desired.

Pecan Tassies

1 C. soft margarine   2-3 oz. pkgs. cream cheese
2 C. sifted flour

Blend thoroughly with hands. Shape into 1″ balls. Press into small cupcake pans, bottom and sides, forming shells. Sprinkle bottom with ½ teaspoon finely chopped pecans. Fill with the following:

2 eggs   1½ C. brown sugar
2 T. melted margarine   1 C. chopped pecans

Bake at 350° for 15 minutes. Reduce heat to 250° and bake for 10 more minutes.

Cherry Delight

CRUST:

½ C. margarine   1 pkg. crushed graham crackers

Mix and press in a 9 x 13″ pan.

1 carton whipped topping   ½ C. powdered sugar

Mix on low. Add 4 ounces, or up to 8 ounces, cream cheese and whip. Put on graham cracker crust. Put 1 or 2 cans of cherry pie filling on top. Refrigerate.

Oreo Cookie Dessert

2 pkgs. instant vanilla pudding
3½ C. cold milk
1-8 oz. pkg. cream cheese

½ stick butter
1 carton whipped topping
1 lb. Oreo cookies

Mix together pudding and milk. Mix separately: cream cheese, butter and whipped topping, then add to pudding mixture. Crush Oreos. Put ⅔ in bottom of an 8 x 8″ pan. Add whipped topping mixture. Sprinkle with remaining Oreo crumbs.

Blueberry Dessert

1-8 oz. pkg. cream cheese
1 C. powdered sugar
1-8 oz. whipped topping

1-14 oz. angel food cake, cut into
   1″ cubes
2-21 oz. cans blueberry pie filling

Beat cream cheese and sugar until smooth; fold in whipped topping and cake. Spread into ungreased 9 x 13″ pan. Top with blueberry pie filling. Refrigerate 4 hours. Cut into squares and serve.

Raspberry Dessert

CRUST:
1 pkg. graham crackers, crushed
¼ C. sugar

⅓ C. margarine, melted

TOPPING:
1 pkg. raspberry gelatin
¼ C. sugar
1 T. lemon juice

1½ C. boiling water
1 pkg. (2 C.) frozen raspberries

FILLING:
3 oz. pkg. cream cheese, softened
⅓ C. powdered sugar

1 tsp. vanilla
1 C. whipped topping

(continued on next page)

Mix together crust ingredients and press into flat pan.

TOPPING: Mix together raspberry gelatin, sugar, lemon juice and boiling water. Add raspberries and stir until dissolved. Refrigerate until slightly thickened.

FILLING: Blend together cream cheese, powdered sugar and vanilla. Add whipped topping. Place cream mixture in graham cracker crust in flat pan. Top with raspberry mixture and refrigerate.

Chocolate Turtle Cheesecake

1-7 oz. pkg. caramels
¼ C. evaporated milk
¾ C. chopped pecans, divided
1-9″ chocolate crumb pie crust
2-3 oz. pkgs. cream cheese,
    softened

½ C. sour cream
1¼ C. milk
1-3.9 oz. pkg. instant chocolate
    pudding mix
½ C. fudge topping

Place caramels and evaporated milk in a heavy saucepan. Heat over medium-low heat, stirring constantly, until smooth (about 5 minutes). Stir in ½ cup chopped pecans. Pour into pie crust. Combine cream cheese, sour cream, and milk in a blender. Process until smooth. Add pudding mix and process for 30 seconds longer. Pour pudding mixture over caramel layer, covering evenly. Chill, covered loosely, until set, about 15 minutes. Drizzle fudge topping over pudding layer in a decorative pattern. Sprinkle top of cake with remaining pecans. Chill, loosely covered, until serving time.

Dirt Cake

2-3 oz. pkgs. instant vanilla
  pudding
3 C. milk
1 stick margarine

8 oz. cream cheese
1 C. powdered sugar
8 oz. whipped topping
1 lb. Oreo cookies

Mix pudding and milk. Fold in whipped topping, margarine, cream cheese adn powdered sugar together. Blend with pudding mixture. Crush Oreo cookies. Alternate layers of cookies and pudding mixture, beginning and ending with crumbs. For a neat idea, do it in a plastic flower pot. Place artificial flowers on top. Garnish with gummy worms; or may use a 9 x 13″ pan, using cookie crumbs on top and bottom layer.

Banana Pudding

1-8 oz. pkg. cream cheese
1-14 oz. can sweetened
   condensed milk
1-5 oz. pkg. instant vanilla pudding mix
3 C. cold milk

1 tsp. vanilla extract
1-8 oz. container frozen whipped
   topping, thawed, divided
½-12 oz. pkg. vanilla wafers
4 bananas, sliced

In a large bowl, beat cream cheese until fluffy. Beat in condensed milk, pudding mix, cold milk and vanilla until smooth. Fold in ½ of the whipped topping. Line the bottom of a 9 x 13″ dish with vanilla wafers. Arrange sliced bananas over wafers. Spread with pudding mixture. Top with remaining whipped topping. Chill.

Self-Filled Cupcakes

1 pkg. devil's food cake mix,
    prepared as directed
1-8 oz. pkg. cream cheese
⅓ C. sugar

1 egg
Dash of salt
1 C. chocolate chips

Fill muffin tins ⅔ full of cake mixture. Cream the cheese with the sugar; beat in egg and salt. Stir in chocolate chips. Drop 1 rounded teaspoonful of mixture into each cupcake. Bake as directed on cake mix. Cupcakes may be frosted or dusted with powdered sugar.

Cheesecake Squares

1 box yellow cake mix
1 stick margarine
1 egg

1-8 oz. pkg. cream cheese
2 C. powdered sugar
2 eggs

To prepare first layer, mix together cake mix, melted margarine and 1 egg. Pat into the bottom of pan. For second layer, mix together cream cheese, powdered sugar and 2 eggs. Pour on top of first layer. Bake at 350° for 40 minutes or until browned. Cool and cut into squares.

Quick and Easy Peanut Butter Pie

1-3 oz. pkg. cream cheese
1 C. powdered sugar
⅓ C. peanut butter

1-8 oz. pkg. whipped topping
1 graham cracker crust

Whip cream cheese until soft and fluffy. Beat in sugar and peanut butter until smooth. Fold whipped topping into peanut butter mixture. Pour into graham cracker crust. Sprinkle with chopped nuts. Chill.

Easy Truffles

1 pkg. Oreos
8 oz. cream cheese

1 lb. vanilla candy coating

Mix Oreos and cream cheese in food processor. Roll into 1″ balls. Melt the vanilla candy coating in a microwave-safe bowl. Dip balls and place on waxed paper to harden.

White Chocolate No-Bake Cheesecake

1 C. white chocolate chips
2-8 oz. pkgs. cream cheese
1-8 oz. whipped topping

1-9″ graham cracker crust
⅓ C. English toffee bits

In a saucepan, melt chips over medium heat; stir until smooth. Take off heat; stir in cream cheese until smooth. Fold in whipped topping. Pour in crust. Cover and refrigerate overnight. Just before serving, sprinkle on toffee.

Cream Cheese Brownies

1 pkg. German chocolate cake mix
8 oz. cream cheese, softened
1 egg

½ C. sugar
½ C. milk chocolate chips

Heat oven to 350°. Grease and flour pan, 15½ x 10½". Prepare cake mix as directed on package. Pour batter into pan. Mix remaining ingredients. Drop by tablespoon onto batter. Cut through batter with knife for marbled effect. Sprinkle additional chocolate chips on top. Bake 25 to 30 minutes or until when pricked with toothpick, it comes out dry.

French Strawberry Pie

1 qt. strawberries, divided
⅔ C. water
1 C. sugar
3 T. cornstarch

⅓ C. water
1-3 oz. pkg. cream cheese,
    softened

Save about ½ cup strawberries for garnish. Combine 1 cup strawberries and ⅔ cup water; simmer together for 3 minutes. Blend together sugar, cornstarch and ⅓ cup water and add to boiling strawberry mixture. Boil for 1 minute, stirring constantly. Cool. Spread bottom of cooled, baked pie shell with the cream cheese. Put remaining strawberries in pie shell. Cover with cooked mixture. Garnish with the reserved strawberries. Refrigerate until firm, about 2 hours. Serve with whipped cream or ice cream.

Cherries in the Snow

6 egg whites
¼ tsp. salt
½ tsp. cream of tartar
1¾ C. sugar
2-3 oz. pkgs. cream cheese

1 C. sugar
1 tsp. vanilla
2 C. whipping cream
2 C. miniature marshmallows

Beat egg whites, salt and cream of tartar to soft peaks. Gradually add sugar, beating until very stiff peaks form and sugar is dissolved. Spread into 9 x 13″ pan and bake at 275° for 1 hour. Turn off heat and let dry in oven, with door closed, overnight. Beat cream cheese, sugar and vanilla until smooth. Whip cream and fold into cheese mixture along with marshmallows. Spread on top of meringue and refrigerate for several hours. Cut into serving pieces and serve with topping.

(continued on next page)

TOPPING:

1 can cherry pie filling
1 tsp. lemon juice

2 C. fresh, sliced strawberries
   or 16 oz. frozen

Mix cherry pie filling, lemon juice and fresh or frozen strawberries. Spoon on top of each serving.

Chocolate Bavarian Torte

1-18¼ oz. pkg. devil's food
    cake mix, without pudding
1-8 oz. pkg. cream cheese,
    softened
⅔ C. packed brown sugar

1 tsp. vanilla
⅛ tsp. salt
2 C. whipping cream, whipped
2 T. grated semi-sweet
    chocolate

Mix and bake cake according to package directions, using two 9″ cake pans. Cool in pans for 15 minutes; remove from pans and cool completely on a wire rack. In a mixing bowl, beat cream cheese, sugar, vanilla and salt until fluffy. Fold in cream. Split each cake into two horizontal layers. Place one layer on a serving plate. Spread on one-fourth of the cream mixture and sprinkle with one-fourth of the chocolate. Repeat layers. Cover and refrigerate for 8 hours or overnight.

Oreo Pudding

1 pkg. Oreo cookies
2 small boxes instant vanilla
    pudding

3½ C. milk
8 oz. cream cheese
1½ C. whipped topping

Crush Oreo cookies and spread half in a 13 x 8″ dish. Mix rest of ingredients; spread over cookies. Top with remaining crumbs.

Frozen Mocha Marbled Dessert

2½ C. crushed Oreo cookies
3 T. melted butter
2-8 oz. pkgs. cream cheese
2-14 oz. cans sweetened
    condensed milk

2 tsp. vanilla
2 C. Rich's topping
2 T. coffee
1 C. chocolate syrup

Mix cookie crumbs and melted butter; press into pan. In a bowl, beat cream cheese, milk and vanilla. Whip 2 cups Rich's topping and fold in with cream cheese mixture. Spoon half of mixture in another bowl and set aside. Add coffee and chocolate syrup to remaining cream cheese mixture. Spoon half of this on cookies. Top with half of cream cheese mixture. Repeat layers. Cut through layers with knife to marbleize. Freeze.

Easy Cherry Cheese Squares

3½ C. graham crackers
⅓ C. butter, melted
½ pt. whipped cream

1-8 oz. pkg. cream cheese
1 C. sugar
1 C. pie filling

Crush graham crackers in a blender or with a rolling pin to 1⅓ cups. Mix crushed graham crackers with melted butter. Press evenly in 8 x 8 x 2″ pan. Bake in oven at 375° for about 5 minutes, or until lightly brown. Let cool. In bowl, beat cream cheese and sugar until well blended. Gently fold in whipped cream. Spread evenly in cooled crust. Top with pie filling. Refrigerate about 2 hours or until chilled. Cut into squares. Double recipe for large cake pan, 13 x 9″.

Pumpkin Pecan Cake Roll

3 eggs
1 C. sugar
¾ C. flour
¾ C. canned pumpkin
1½ tsp. cinnamon
1 tsp. baking powder

1 tsp. ginger
½ tsp. salt
½ tsp. nutmeg
1 tsp. lemon juice
1 C. finely chopped pecans
Confectioners' sugar

FILLING:
2-3 oz. pkgs. cream cheese, softened
¼ C. margarine, softened

1 C. confectioners' sugar
½ tsp. vanilla

(continued on next page)

Line a greased 15 x 10 x 1″ baking pan with waxed paper and grease the paper; set aside. In a mixing bowl, beat eggs for 5 minutes. Add sugar, flour, pumpkin, cinnamon, baking powder, ginger, salt and nutmeg; mix well. Add lemon juice. Spread batter evenly in prepared pan; sprinkle with pecans. Bake at 375° for 15 minutes or until cake springs back when lightly touched. Cool for 5 minutes. Turn cake onto a kitchen towel dusted with confectioners' sugar. Gently peel off waxed paper. Roll up cake in towel, jelly roll-style, starting with a short side. Cool completely on wire rack. In a mixing bowl, combine filling ingredients; beat until smooth. Unroll cake; spread filling on cake to within ½″ of edges. Roll up again; place seam side down on a serving platter. Cover and refrigerate for at least 1 hour before serving.

Index

Appetizers